Praise for The Illustrated Book of Cat Phrases

"Five stars! I was so intrigued, I paused my 16-hour nap schedule to read it. 'The Illustrated Book of Cat Phrases' is the purr-fect read for those long afternoons in the sunbeam."

– Whiskers McFluff

"This book had me meowling with laughter! It's like a laser pointer for the brain - I just couldn't look away."

– Sir Pounce-a-lot

"An uproarious romp through the feline lexicon. It's simply the cat's meow. I would've clawed at it, but I respect literature too much."

– Gabo

"Absolutely hiss-terical! I haven't had this much fun since I knocked that expensive vase off the counter. A must-read for any kitty looking to expand their linguistic repertoire."

– Mr. Snibbley

"I give it two paws up—and I would have given it a third if I had one. It's the kind of book that makes you purr with delight and then leave it strategically on the floor for your human to trip over."

– Mittens von Cattenstein

"The section on 'cat naps' really spoke to me on a spiritual level. I read it in between my third and fourth nap of the day. This book is the purr-fect excuse to cozy up on your human's keyboard."

– Bytes the Bookworm

"Finally, a book that speaks to my feline soul. I laughed so hard, I coughed up a hairball. It's a literary furball of wisdom every cat should cough—er, cough up. I mean, pick up!"

– Binx the Tabby

The Illustrated Book of Cat Phrases

Brian Medrano

RED GATES
— PUBLISHING —

To our feline friends and those who care for them

The Illustrated Book of Cat Phrases
Visit our socials @redgatespublishing
Visit the author's website at www.brianmedrano.com
First Edition: April 2024
ISBN: 978-1-951383-05-3
Red Gates Publishing - Los Angeles, CA 90020
Cover Design by Mariana Reyes

This book was published in the United States of America.

The characters and events depicted in this book are fictitious. Any similarity to actual persons, living or dead, or actual events is purely coincidental.

Cover and book illustrations: All images were created by generative artificial intelligence using OpenAI's Dalle3

Image prompts, editing and design by Brian Medrano

Table of Contents

Fat cat

Definition

Refers to a wealthy, powerful person, often used in a derogatory sense.

Origin

The term "fat cat" originated in the 1920s in the United States as a political term for wealthy individuals who heavily funded political campaigns, indicating their significant influence in politics. Over time, by the mid-20th century, its use broadened to describe any affluent person, particularly those seen as greedy or disconnected from common people. This shift reflected growing concerns about income inequality and corporate dominance. In modern usage, "fat cat" commonly refers to wealthy executives or powerful individuals, often with negative connotations of greed, corruption, and social irresponsibility.

Example

Environmental activists accused the fat cats in the oil industry of prioritizing profits over the planet's health.

Cat got your tongue?

Definition

Asked when someone is unusually quiet, suggesting they are at a loss for words.

Origin

The phrase "cat got your tongue?" has an uncertain origin with several theories. One links it to the "Cat-o'-Nine-Tails" whip used in the British Navy, suggesting that a flogged person might be too pained to speak. Another theory ties it to medieval superstitions where cats, associated with witches, were believed to steal voices.

Example

During the heated debate, when he suddenly fell silent, I couldn't resist taunting, "Cat got your tongue, or are you out of arguments?"

Look what the cat dragged in

Definition

Used humorously to refer to someone's arrival, often implying they look disheveled or are unwelcome.

Origin

Cats, of course, have a natural instinct to hunt and bring home their "catches." This often includes dead or half-dead creatures like mice, birds, or squirrels. These "gifts" were probably not always welcomed by their human owners.

While the phrase was initially used quite literally, its meaning has broadened over time. It can now be used to describe:

- Someone arriving unwelcome or unexpectedly.
- Something surprising or shocking.
- Something messy or troublesome.
- Even someone or something unpleasant or distasteful.

Example

When he stumbled into the office late and disheveled, his coworker greeted him with a smirk, saying, "Look what the cat dragged in!"

A cat nap

Definition

A short, light sleep, similar to the brief naps cats take.

Origin

The Likely Culprit: Kitty Behavior
The most widely accepted explanation for "cat nap"
draws inspiration directly from our feline friends. Cats
are renowned for their ability to sleep throughout the
day in short bursts, often curled up in cozy spots. This
frequent napping likely resonated with humans who
also experience the need for occasional daytime energy
boosts.

Example

Alex found that a quick cat nap in his home office was
the perfect remedy for the mid-afternoon slump.

Raining cats and dogs

Definition

Used to describe particularly heavy rain.

Origin

The Norse Mythology Mix:
One theory comes from Norse mythology, where Odin, the all-father, was often accompanied by wolves and dogs, representing wind and storms. Some suggest the heavy rain and strong winds of these stormy tales might have given rise to the image of raining dogs.

The Literal Liftoff:
This theory suggests the phrase originated from observing debris swept away by heavy rain. In medieval times, streets were often filthy, and a downpour could easily carry dead animals, including small creatures like cats and dogs.

The Lost in Translation Tango:
This theory proposes that "raining cats and dogs" might be a corruption of the ancient Greek word "katadoupoi," which referred to waterfalls. Over time, and through possible language evolution, "katadoupoi" could have morphed into the more vivid and relatable imagery of raining animals.

Example

We were shopping in town when suddenly it began raining cats and dogs, forcing everyone to pack up and run for shelter.

Not a cat in hell's chance

Definition

Something has absolutely no chance of happening.

Origin

The phrase likely emerged in the mid-20th century, specifically within the United States.

Combination of metaphors: This posits that it's a fusion of the idea of hell being a terrible place and cats possessing remarkable agility and resourcefulness. Combining these concepts results in the powerful image of even a skilled cat failing miserably in hell.

Evolution of an earlier phrase: Some suggest it might have evolved from other existing idioms with similar meanings, like "not a snowball's chance in hell."

Example

Trying to get a last-minute reservation at that popular restaurant? There's not a cat in hell's chance on a Friday night.

To throw the cat among the pigeons

Definition

Another way of saying causing trouble or disruption, especially by revealing something controversial.

Origin

There's evidence that putting a cat in a dovecote might have been a colonial-era pastime in India. People might have even placed bets on how many pigeons the cat could catch.

Example

Bringing up the controversial topic at the family dinner was akin to throwing the cat among the pigeons, sparking heated debates.

Like herding cats

Definition

Describes an attempt to control or organize a group of people who are unmanageable or chaotic.

Origin

These furry felines are notoriously independent and have a strong aversion to being controlled. Their unpredictable nature and agility make it incredibly difficult to corral them in a desired direction, hence the comparison to managing a seemingly impossible task.

A Monty Python Connection:

Some attribute the popularization of the phrase to the British comedy troupe Monty Python. In their 1979 film "Life of Brian," a group of shepherds jokingly discuss herding "flocks of cats" instead of sheep, highlighting the absurdity of such a task.

Example

Wrangling the five toddlers into the car for the grocery trip was like herding cats.

Cat's eyes in the dark

Definition

A feeling of unease, suspicion, or being watched.

Origin

The most straightforward interpretation takes the phrase at face value. Cats, thanks to their tapetum lucidum, a reflective layer in their eyes, can see exceptionally well in low light. Their eyes often gleam in the dark, which might have led to the observation of "seeing the cat's eyes in the dark."

In many cultures, cats are associated with hidden knowledge, foresight, or even supernatural abilities.

Gaining hidden insight or understanding: The cat's glowing eyes symbolize hidden truths or mysteries that are revealed to those observants enough to perceive them.

Example

The detective's relentless questioning finally pierced the facade, and for a fleeting moment, I saw the cat's eyes in the dark – a flicker of fear that betrayed the suspect's carefully crafted story.

A cat may look at a king

Definition

A phrase that challenges the rigid social hierarchies of the time. By comparing a lowly cat to a powerful king, it subtly suggests that everyone, regardless of their social standing, has the inherent right to observe and even question those in positions of authority.

Origin

Over time, the proverb's meaning has evolved somewhat. While retaining its core message of basic rights, it has shifted to represent the idea that everyone has the freedom to form their own opinions and express them, even if they differ from those in power. It can also symbolize the right to observe and critique societal norms and customs, challenging the status quo and advocating for change.

Example

Even though she was just an intern, she voiced her opinion boldly to the CEO during the all hands meeting, proving that a cat may look at a king.

Cat with gloves catches no mice

Definition

Excessive caution or over-refinement can hinder one's ability to achieve their goals. It's used to encourage taking risks and embracing a more proactive approach.

Origin

Possible Inspiration: Some scholars suggest the proverb may have been inspired by Aesop's fable of the Fox and the Cat, where the cautious cat misses out on the hunt while the fox, despite lacking claws, uses its cunning to catch prey.

Example

Abigail realized that to succeed in the cutthroat world of politics, a cat in gloves catches no mice, and decided to be more outspoken.

Cat's pajamas

Definition

Something or someone as excellent, of the highest quality, or highly desirable. It can refer to both material items and people.

Origin

The exact origin of this phrase is a bit murky, but it seems to have emerged in the early 1920s in the United States.

New Fashion Trends: Some believe it arose during a time of exciting fashion changes, particularly the introduction of more comfortable and stylish pajamas for men. The comfortable "cat's meow" pajamas might have stood out compared to traditional sleepwear, earning the playful moniker.

Evolution: Initially applied to pajamas, the expression quickly broadened to encompass anything considered outstanding, becoming a popular term during the Roaring Twenties and beyond. While still in use today, "cat's pajamas" is considered slightly antiquated.

Example

His new jazz album is the cat's pajamas - it's got everyone talking!

When the cat's away the mice will play

Definition

People are more likely to engage in carefree or mischievous behavior when someone in a position of authority is absent. It highlights the tendency for people to shirk responsibility or break rules when they believe they won't face consequences.

Origin

Ancient Roots: The concept of this proverb has existed for centuries, with similar expressions found in ancient cultures around the world.

Latin Inspiration: The most direct ancestor of the English phrase is believed to be a medieval Latin proverb, "Dum felis dormit, mus gaudet et exsi litantro," which translates to "While the cat sleeps, the mouse rejoices and leaps out of its hole."

Example
As soon as the boss left the office early, the staff started a game of ping-pong, proving that when the cat's away, the mice will play.

Cool cat

Definition

Someone who is stylish, confident, and composed. It signifies someone who possesses effortless coolness and navigates life with a relaxed, easygoing vibe.

Origin

The term first appeared in the 1940s within the African American jazz scene. Jazz musicians used "cool" to describe music that was mellow, sophisticated, and emotionally detached, as opposed to the hot, aggressive style of swing. This notion of "cool" then seeped into language, and "cool cat" emerged as a way to describe individuals embodying this particular attitude.

Popularity and Variations: Through the 1950s and 60s, "cool cat" exploded in popularity, appearing in movies, music, and pop culture. It spawned numerous variations like "hip cat," "slick cat," and "groovy cat," each adding slightly different nuances to the core meaning.

Example

She strutted into the room with her shades on, a total cool cat.

No room to swing a cat

Definition

A space is incredibly small and crowded.
Feeling overwhelmed or suffocated.

Origin

Naval slang: Perhaps sailors on cramped ships, where
whipping tails of the "cat-o'-nine-tails" (a punishment
tool) could barely find room to swing, coined the
phrase.

General reference to cats: Others believe it simply arose
from the image of a playful feline needing ample space
to stretch and pounce.

Example

With three deadlines looming and a sick child at home,
my life felt like there was no room to swing a cat.

Curiosity killed the cat

Definition

Venturing into the unknown can lead to negative consequences.

Origin

The exact origin of this saying is not clear, with traces back to the 16th century. Various European versions existed, highlighting the potential dangers of excessive curiosity. These early proverbs often included animals like foxes or mice, but it was the "cat" version that stuck in English-speaking cultures.

Modern invention: The full phrase, "curiosity killed the cat but satisfaction brought it back," likely emerged in the late 20th or early 21st century. It seems to be a contemporary addition to the traditional proverb, aiming to offer a more balanced and optimistic perspective on curiosity.

Example

Pablo couldn't resist snooping through the confidential files, but as they say, curiosity killed the cat, and he was soon caught.

Copycat

Definition

Someone who mimicked others' actions or writing, often in a playful or derogatory way. The term's meaning broadened to encompass more sophisticated forms of imitation, including plagiarism and deliberate copying of ideas or products.

Origin

While the exact origin is unclear, evidence of "copycat" appears in the late 19th century in the United States. The earliest written record comes from 1887, found in Constance Cary Harrison's "Bar Harbor Days," a quasi-memoir. She writes, "Our boys say you are a copycat, if you write in anything that's been already printed." Similar phrases existed for mimicking animals, like "monkey see, monkey do," suggesting "copycat" may have sprung from observing playful imitation.

Variations: The phrase has spawned related terms like "copypasta" (online copied text) and "copycat crime" (imitating criminal acts).

Example

Several copycat restaurants have opened, trying to replicate the famous chef's unique recipes.

Bell the cat

Definition

Someone needs to take the initiative and face potential risks for the greater good.

Origin

The proverb likely originated in the Middle Ages, with similar ideas appearing in various European cultures. One of the earliest recorded versions is found in an animal fable attributed to Aesop, titled "The Mice in Council." In this story, the mice discuss how to deal with a dangerous cat and decide to put a bell around its neck to warn them of its approach. However, no mouse volunteers to perform the risky task of attaching the bell.

Example

Everyone thought the plan was flawed, but it seemed no one was brave enough to bell the cat and confront the leader.

More than one way to skin a cat

Definition

There's more than one method to achieve a goal, even if it can sound unconventional or surprising.

Origin

The exact origin remains murky, but the earliest known written reference dates to the 19th century in the United States. Some speculate it evolved from older sayings with similar meanings, like "There are more ways to kill a dog than hanging" (1678).

Variations: French: "Il y a plusieurs façons de faire cuire un œuf" (There are many ways to cook an egg)

Spanish: "Hay más de un camino a Roma" (There are more than one road to Rome)

Italian: "Non c'è una sola strada per arrivare in cima" (There is not only one way to reach the top)

Example

When the negotiations stalled, he smiled and said, 'Remember, there's more than one way to skin a cat,' and proposed a new deal.

Let the cat out of the bag

Definition

To reveal a secret or surprise unintentionally, often with unexpected or damaging consequences.

Origin

While the exact origin is not known there are several possible theories.

Medieval Market Scam: One theory claims it originated from a shady practice in medieval marketplaces. Vendors would replace a pig purchase with a cat hidden in the bag, tricking unsuspecting buyers. Revealing the cat would be akin to "letting the cat out of the bag."

Sailor's Tale: Another theory suggests it arose from nautical life. Sailors who tattled on their comrades were said to be "letting the cat out of the bag" used to punish transgressors. The "cat" here referred to the instrument used for flogging.

Example

I was trying to keep the party a surprise, but my little brother accidentally let the cat out of the bag.

Quiet as a cat

Definition

Someone or something making very little noise, like a stealthy feline stalking its prey.

Origin

While not pinpointed to a specific date, the phrase emerged sometime in the early 1920s in the United States. Likely inspired by the rising fashion trend of comfortable pajamas resembling feline attire, "cat's pajamas" became a popular slang term for excellence.

Example

In the library, she was quiet as a cat, carefully selecting her books without a sound.

In a cat birdseat

Definition

To be in an enviable position, one with significant advantage or control. It often signifies having the upper hand in a situation or competition.

Origin

Bird Connection: The most common explanation ties it to the gray catbird, a North American songbird known for its diverse repertoire and tendency to perch high in trees. This interpretation suggests that being "in the catbird seat" refers to the bird's advantageous position, surveying the situation from above.

Example

Business: "After securing the major investor, the startup was in the catbird seat to dominate the market."

Politics: "With strong poll numbers and key endorsements, the incumbent candidate is in the catbird seat for re-election."

Metaphorical: "Knowing all the characters' secrets, the writer felt in the catbird seat to craft a compelling story."

Cat's cradle

Definition

A children's string game; can also refer to a complex or convoluted, or interconnected situation.

Origin

The String Game: This refers to a traditional game where players loop a string around their fingers and hands, manipulating it to create various intricate patterns and shapes. It involves collaboration and dexterity, requiring players to work together to form specific figures.

Example

Trying to negotiate this international treaty is like unraveling a cat's cradle. There are so many hidden clauses and interconnected interests.

Dead cat bounce

Definition

A short-lived and temporary price increase in a declining trend, most commonly used in finance but also applicable to other contexts. It carries the implication that the rise won't last and is ultimately meaningless in the larger downward trajectory.

Origin

While the exact origin is unclear, the phrase likely stems from the dark humor proverb: "Even a dead cat will bounce if it falls from high enough."

Finance:
In the stock market, it refers to a stock experiencing a brief upward swing after a significant decline, often mistaken for a potential trend reversal. However, the price typically resumes its downward journey soon after.

Example

After dropping 20% in a week, the stock saw a dead cat bounce today, but analysts remain cautious about its long-term prospects.

Playing with a kitten's tail

Definition

Engaging in a seemingly harmless activity that might lead to trouble.

Origin

Likely stems from observations of cat behavior. Kittens can be playful and enjoy gentle tail touches, but when overly stimulated, they might suddenly turn defensive and hiss or swat.

Alternative phrases:

Stirring the hornet's nest

Poking a bear with a stick

Opening a can of worms

Example

The journalist hoped her investigative report would expose corruption, but she worried she was just playing with a kitten's tail - antagonizing powerful figures without causing real change.

Conceited as a barber's cat

Definition

Describes someone who exhibits excessive pride and vanity.

Origin

The exact origin not known, but its presence dates to at least the late 19th century.

Barber as a social hub: Barbershops were traditional gathering places for men, where discussions and opinions flowed freely. A cat residing in such an environment might develop a sense of self-importance due to constant exposure to conversations and admiration.
Refined appearance: Barbers often took pride in their grooming skills, extending their care to resident cats, resulting in well-kept felines who might develop a conceited air.
Symbolic association: Cats are often depicted as independent and aloof creatures, traits sometimes associated with conceit.

Example

Nick walked around with his nose held high, conceited as a barber's cat, after winning the office trivia contest.

Cat with nine lives

Definition

Someone who seems to have an uncanny ability to avoid harm or misfortune and repeatedly escape dangerous situations. It implies someone with remarkable resilience, resourcefulness, and the ability to bounce back from challenges.

Origin

The exact origin is unclear, but theories point to several possibilities:

Ancient Egypt: Egyptians revered cats as sacred beings, possibly associating their agility and survival skills with multiple lives.
European folklore: Myths and proverbs across Europe mention cats having multiple lives, sometimes attributing the number nine to its mystical significance.
Scientific observations: Cats' incredible flexibility and dexterity, allowing them to land safely from falls, might have inspired the belief in "nine lives."

Example

He's a cat with nine lives, that one! He's walked away from more accidents than I can count.

Catcall

Definition

Shouting harassing and frequently sexually suggestive, threatening, or mocking remarks at someone in a public setting.

Less common: A loud or raucous shout or cry, typically expressing disapproval at a performance, event, or speaker.

Origin

Unclear origin as it aligns with the use of "catcalls" in theater or sporting events where the audience might voice disapproval through whistles, shouts, or jeers.

Tex Avery Cartoons (Possible Influence): The 1940s cartoons by Tex Avery, particularly those featuring a leering wolf character who whistles at women, might have popularized the idea of using whistles and suggestive behavior as a form of "flirting."

Example

Sarah hurried down the street, wishing she could avoid the inevitable catcalling from the construction workers across the road.

Landing on one's feet like a cat

Definition

The ability to recover quickly from difficulties or to adapt to new situations with ease.

Origin

Folklore: Across various cultures, cats are often associated with having multiple lives or possessing magical abilities to avoid harm. This symbolism transferred to the phrase, emphasizing someone's seemingly impossible knack for escaping misfortune.

Observation: Cats' remarkable flexibility and agility allow them to land safely from falls, often seeming to contort their bodies mid-air. This natural ability inspired the metaphor for humans who overcome challenges with similar grace and resourcefulness.

Example

Despite losing her job, Sarah landed on her feet like a cat. She started a successful freelance business and ended up happier and more fulfilled than before.

Lost kitten

Definition

Someone who seems helpless, lost, and in need of assistance.

Origin

Likely emerged from the natural concern and desire to help a young animal in distress.

Example

Feeling overwhelmed on her first day of college, Maya wandered the campus like a lost kitten as she searched for her chemistry lab.

Playing cat and mouse

Definition

A suspenseful back-and-forth with no clear winner.

Origin

The idiom comes from the natural world and the hunting behavior of domestic cats. Cats often capture small prey like mice, but instead of killing them right away, they might bat them around and play with them for a while.

Example

The hacker enjoyed playing cat and mouse with the cybersecurity team, leaving behind taunting messages before disappearing again.

Eyes like a kitten

Definition

Used to portray someone's eyes as endearing, captivating, and possibly hinting at a hint of youthful innocence or mischief.

Origin

It likely arose organically from people using kittens as a relatable comparison to describe certain eye characteristics.

Example

The little girl looked at me with eyes like a kitten, clearly up to something but too adorable to reprimand.

All cats are grey in the dark

Definition

In suggests that in situations where there's a lack of clarity or information, distinctions become unimportant.

The dark, physical appearance is unimportant. Sometimes used in a vulgar and offensive context.

Origin

The exact origin is not clear as many cultures used similar phrases.

Early uses in books:

John Heywood's Book of Proverbs in 1547 and Don Quixote by Miguel de Cervantes in 1605.

Example

With so little evidence, it's impossible to say who's guilty. All cats are grey in the dark with these accusations flying around.

Like a cat on a tin roof

Definition

Used to describe someone who is uneasy, agitated, or nervous.

Origin

While the exact origin is unclear, it likely stemmed from the natural tendency of cats to dislike hot surfaces and the precarious footing a tin roof would provide.

Similar version: Like a cat on hot bricks

The phrase gained wider recognition due to the famous play by Tennessee Williams, "Cat on a Hot Tin Roof" (1955). The play's title and themes perfectly capture the essence of the idiom.

Example

With the interview approaching, Sarah paced the room, feeling like a cat on a hot tin roof, worrying about every possible question.

Please leave a review

If you liked this book, please consider leaving a review on Amazon! Bonus if you include a photo of your cat.

Pls?

Also by Brian Medrano

Creepy Pumpkin Patch: A spooky, fun story for imaginative readers

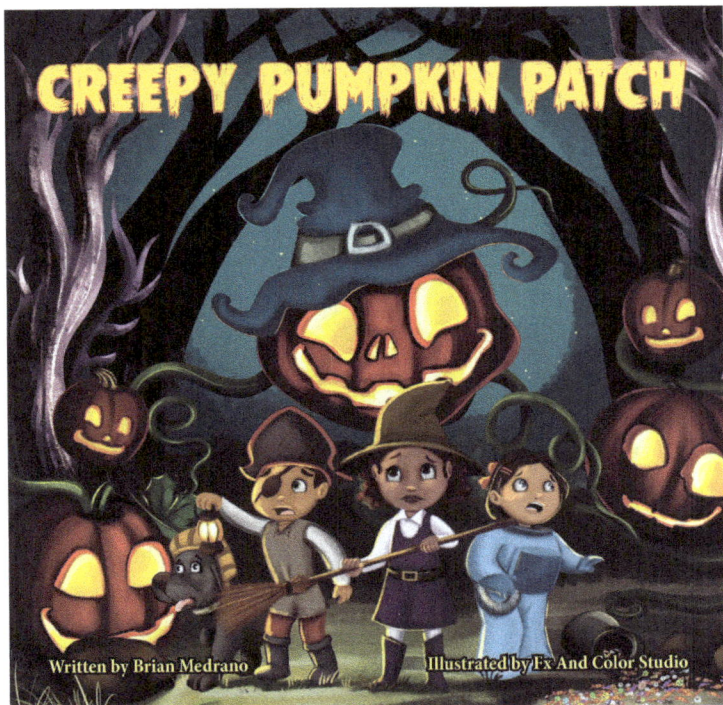

www.ingramcontent.com/pod-product-compliance
Lightning Source LLC
LaVergne TN
LVHW021122080426
835513LV00011B/1207